The Dementia of Language

*

Sara Toruño-Conley

FUTURECYCLE PRESS

www.futurecycle.org

Published by FutureCycle Press

Lexington, Kentucky, USA

ISBN 978-1-938853-89-0

Contents

For my mother, Caren Ann Miller

Prologue

The first sign was your handwriting. Like a child's
it slanted left then right, letters unevenly placed,
lines falling off. The endearing attempt made.

Everything else was normal.
You drove by yourself 433 miles, sometimes along the coast.
You maneuvered up hills casually taken for granted,
created self-portraits along the cliffs, ate at cafés,
ordered exactly what you wanted.

Life is easy at this stage. Handwriting is hardly used,
barely noticed. Words
are still pronounced easily; you recall names
of childhood friends and solve complex formulas,
problems left finished.
We barely noticed.

Part 1: The Daughter's Poem

Growing Neurons in the Desert

Her ideas are now like fog in an awkward desert,
though she's never been good with reason:

this idea she had—to plant a garden in the Mojave,
watch it grow with little water, watch it
perform miracles, watch the neurons sprout
from little to nothing, appearing as a storm, a tornado.

The doctors have said these will never come back,
it will never come back, but the garden grows
in the back yard by the patch of dead grass.

The order is gone; the fog remains
over the widely spaced creosote bushes of the Mojave.

Remembering Swim Lessons

Don't forget to pack Mother's clothes,
a toothbrush, socks. Wrinkles

are okay; they remain distinguishing
under the light, indentations
of each labored conversation,
the new difficulty of language. Her love.

But tell her not to worry:
two plus two still equals four although
it's the attempt that matters, not the outcome.
Remind her that silence is often a blessing.

When she gets here, we'll go swimming and burn
and cry, and remind her

that Tuesdays used to be swim lessons, mother driving
us children in the dry heat,
our little faces incapable of reaching into the future.

If you had never lost your mind, would you still garden
in the dry soil every day, keeping yourself busy?

If you were a dream, would you
slip your clothes on backwards,
leave the dishes out,
fall off your dialogue, let the birds feed
in leftover puddles?

If this is a dream, how wonderful to be of one seed,
our bodies curved toward the sky, waiting.

The vampire mistakes the dog's name for mine:
how my mother created me
and now dismembers me, struggling to remember

when Thanksgiving comes every year
though she can't remember the word "feast."

She used to have a young smile, a body that held
her children in a desert valley with little souls
driving to Stater Bros. for last-minute butter:

the people remembering nothing
in fear of insanity sifting them over
the snow-covered mountains,

the vampire and my father
both desert dwellers, the two of them forgetting
why they moved here, having a feast
with the others.

Wouldn't it be easier, if it took us all,
than the creeping antimatter of this place?

Sometimes you're drunk
in my dreams: the bartender slipped us something,
made you have to drive us home in the awkward night.

You go in circles,
say there's turkey in the fridge from Thanksgiving.
Thanksgiving was months ago. You're a woman again,
a human, a mother; you speak so eloquently

but, more importantly, logically.
This feels real, driving in circles,
complaining about the margaritas we drank, forgetting
where we came from or what you are.

After the Wedding

You think she's slipping;
she'll agree with anyone. She'll believe
she has blue eyes and stood over the Grand Canyon

if you tell her. She danced anyway.
She still loves movement clinging to her
as leftover dreams.
Though she went to bed early, she remembered

to call and apologize. She remembered
to laugh. Soon, you'll be spoon-feeding her,
hiding her, encouraging bits of her,
likes and dislikes, to turn to ashes.

She danced the first hour. She knows all our faces.
This must be the worst kind of pain
to try to sound out each half syllable,
half a memory.

Part 2: The Father's Poem

The First to Fly

A patchwork of city lights,
a man falls asleep waiting for the middle
his wife has forgotten.

Looking out the window
they both think they must have been terrified,
the first to invent.

Invention becomes a way to avoid death
when that sliver of humanity falls from the plane.
She'll be waiting for a new one.

She'll invent a new language.

The Wedding Reception

I lived
years ago when we were young,
too young, a brilliant glow from our faces

staring into a hollowed-out oak tree, bark peeling
from the core. The long
journey up. Not until I was old
did I settle for ordinary.

Youth filled us with proverbs, filled us
with wonderful lies. So now I say,
let the old woman dance:

she might remember that endless filling;
let her kiss the young boy, someone's nephew, someone's
brother. Let the night kiss all the boys so we may forget.

A Forgotten Vacation

There's color in the sides
of your eye,
the side of the ocean along Mexico.
Sides represent memory;
these are where they're discarded,
the alphabet. I'm an old man

dancing until death.
The tourists laugh and take pictures;
you would laugh, too. I'm certain of it.
Not because you're cruel,
but for other reasons.

I also have forgotten symbols, but I
remember color like your favorite color red,
such passion for such a little person,
and I mean that lovingly. This

is where our trip ends: me,
the dancing man, you.
I'll be bent over, folded,
scorched when we fly home.
Not from the loss of memory;
from memory itself.

On the Way to Church

I've fed you, clothed you, reminded you of the god
you knew as a child, bathed you in your Easter Sunday
white dress, reminded you of your father
moving in staccato towards the car, followed by
his three faithful daughters.

I've helped you recall this,
shamefully, but for the sake of your comfort.

And what is comfort but an arid landscape? Wife,
if I've ever known you,
this is all we have at the end.

Your arm caught between
the sofa and the wall, what else could you do?
You fell asleep.

Cried *my lost family,* forgot the reason for crying,
remembered the pain.

The memory of making popcorn for your children
in your bare feet, dropping kernels on the kitchen floor,
being able to laugh so easily,
loving calculus on Sunday mornings.

Weeks later your arm is bruised,
and I've almost lost you.

When I die
I want that one song,
the one by John

Lemon. You catch the last syllable, let it die,
and correct yourself.

Pools are relaxing,
the water's too cold, but the night sky
is electric.
New memories found.

We ate at a Mexican restaurant
in the airport. I helped you lift a shrimp taco.
I sipped.

We laughed and were silent.
I'm tired when I'm with you,
remembering things to say.

Without you, I've only been half made.

Part 3: The Afflicted

The Dementia of Language

Forgetting is the opposite of absence,
a whirlpool in which those forgetful grasp at logic,
only to fail:

Today there was this thing,
You know, my daughter crying laughter,
saying Dad is coming home.
He went, you know.
He went somewhere, huge mountains over there.
A crowd of children looking at the sky, planes
flying overhead, what do you eat on?
What did I eat? Where did I land? Those beautiful colored birds,
a desert bigger than our desert, a tree without leaves,
a place where you eat, a place where you sleep. I went there

like a break in dry soil,
a parting of the clouds.

Helping her mother sound syllables,
the memory of a poem.

A Love Poem

I once was young, the length
of my fingers extending into the ocean,

forming my moon.
I asked you to the Sadie Hawkins
dance; you said yes.
I thought I had found it;

then we changed.
But think of the little moments
flying over storms together, developing quickly,

rounding out after the collision, the formation
of my core. Your cruelty

birthed my canyons.
We planted seeds, gave up pleasures,
followed the rotation of bodies.

Still, your two sides are worse than any birth
or death. Can you blame me
for what's happened?

I am still able to speak the way I dream,
a stream of abstract, fully relevant thought.
I've only forgotten your name.

Your face is still concrete as my routine, my feeding
of the dog, the bird's chirp from the clock
above the kitchen window,

noticing the way the leaves brush
against the glass. I am still able to think of time
as linear, to remember
what I ate for breakfast, to think of breakfast
as a morning activity. I am still

able to think of love as a verb
when remembering faces. I still laugh
at the same jokes.

Yet I don't understand why the days have changed.
Voices are calloused; people
move quickly as though I'm a thought to be forgotten.

The knobs on the stove have been removed.

Morning Prayer

The morning after any dream
is a lonely one,
but I don't know why
chimneys are left
soiled. The children continue to feed

as another rolls over in the night. I touch her.

She lets pieces fall
from the empty bookshelf; I used to read
until I no longer inhabited my body. This
wasn't so long ago. If we become children

in the morning, by night our faces will remain,
but I miss our mothers, I miss our daughters we never knew.
Sometimes I feel so simple that
I forget my name.

My Mutation

I've overheard you speaking candidly about our trip
from sometime long ago,
how I displayed the organization of a god:

But what has she become? What new person, now?

If memory is humanity, have I vanished?
I still remember fragments, the long unrest
of the mind, the trip
across state through the smallest of moments,
my daughter with her long, dark ponytail,
a straight line down her back,

the leftover drapes and folds from years past.
If I am this new person or the missing of a person,
I am still your mother.

Today is your day

I was so sure what that meant: "day" is a word
that means confusion, long extended suns
beating down the front door. So is it not logical
to believe you would come for me
before the sun set?

But you're confused

If logic is not my strong point, don't explain,
leave me in the same position, leave me
as I sleep it all away.
It will make sense in the morning
when your offer will not exist.

Then I think all I want is you
and millions of people bundled together
in longing, missing something they've forgotten.
Other times, sweetly, you'll say *let's go*

Let's drive beyond

and I'll want nothing at all, no thought,
a body in such composure.
Leave them behind.

Go without me.

Laments on the Way to Barstow

What is it that makes you human?
Memories? Reminders that to be human
is to be in between?

I sound pessimistic, but I'm really anything
but—I'm neither emotion, only fear
that I'll remember I've forgotten your name.

A few months ago I almost burned the house
away; yes, I'm exaggerating.
But my life must be a constant hyperbole.

That's all that's left.
They took my license; you
told me to relearn second grade math.
Now we go for long drives

to places I can't remember. We drive in the desert,
I know that much.
We drive with the Joshua trees at our backs
and your barely human mother in the passenger seat.

A Proclamation

You've told me I am the embodiment of innocence, incapable
of harm, unknowing of the degree of despair.

I protest that I am still human. I am not
a memory for you
to tug at when thinking of the kind of mother you want to be.

I know humanity
as the methodic rhythm of my everyday life. I know the fear
in waking, attending to the ceremony, relearning
crochet, throwing away,
calling you every day
to proclaim I can't remember.

Is there innocence in fear? If so, perhaps I am.
Though I can cause more harm than you'll ever know.

Epilogue

At three thousand feet,
she plants the Yucca gently
next to the dead lawn.

She falls asleep on
the tattered sofa, her mind
like melting snow, still a god.

She forgets to check
the bed for shadows, strangers
she used to embrace.

Spring is hardly touched
and the winds have ceased this year,
the desert a forgetting.

Why do you age like the seasons, inevitable,
without remembrance?
Last winter, a nonexistent moment for you,
pipes frozen over and forgotten.

You remind me of the process of aging,
the rest of humanity not stuck in a child-like
abandonment of time. But how beautiful

you are as you try to button up your coat,
noticing frost on the window, feathery patterns,
this new phenomenon:

a new winter, a first winter.

The last winter.

Acknowledgments

The following poems first appeared in *Found: Fiction and Poetry Anthology* (Wordrunner eChapbooks, September 2012): "In the Beginning," "The Aftermath" (originally titled "Mother's Aftermath"), and "Growing Neurons in the Desert."

Cover photo, "Cactus" by Brigitte Werner; author photo by Seamus Conley; cover and interior book design by Diane Kistner; Trebuchet text with Bradley Hand titling

About FutureCycle Press

FutureCycle Press is dedicated to publishing lasting English-language poetry books, chapbooks, and anthologies in both print-on-demand and ebook formats. Founded in 2007 by long-time independent editor/publishers and partners Diane Kistner and Robert S. King, the press incorporated as a nonprofit in 2012. A number of our editors are distinguished poets and writers in their own right, and we have been actively involved in the small press movement going back to the early seventies.

The FutureCycle Poetry Book Prize and honorarium is awarded annually for the best full-length volume of poetry we publish in a calendar year. Introduced in 2013, our Good Works projects are anthologies devoted to issues of universal significance, with all proceeds donated to a related worthy cause. Our Selected Poems series highlights contemporary poets with a substantial body of work to their credit; with this series we strive to resurrect work that has had limited distribution and is now out of print.

We are dedicated to giving all of the authors we publish the care their work deserves, making our catalog of titles the most diverse and distinguished it can be, and paying forward any earnings to fund more great books.

We've learned a few things about independent publishing over the years. We've also evolved a unique, resilient publishing model that allows us to focus mainly on vetting and preserving for posterity the most books of exceptional quality without becoming overwhelmed with bookkeeping and mailing, fundraising activities, or taxing editorial and production "bubbles." To find out more about what we are doing, come see us at www.futurecycle.org.

www.ingramcontent.com/pod-product-compliance
Lightning Source LLC
Chambersburg PA
CBHW060047050426
42448CB00012B/3139